I0568879

Revolution and Sugarcane

It All Belongs

Tara Lingeman

Bishop Street Books

Detroit, MI 2025

ISBN: 979-8-218-68034-3

Dedication

For my late friend Sean MacDowell, a far superior poet, who always encouraged my ramblings. I offer a few kernels of his wisdom here:

"Who wants to get an oil change and return empties, when you can read Rilke?"

"Life is very painful. It's advantageous to confront it in all its forms."

"May we be brave enough to have our hearts broken at 80!"

Table of Contents

What can a poem even do?

She asked,
what can a poem
even do?

Can these bars block
ICE from entering,
create shelter during
climate disasters,
stockpile birth control,
approve hormone therapy,
or keep my name off the list?

What can a poem
even do?

Can it lift this dark cloud
of hyper-masculinity
raining down dominance,
throwing its weight around,
chanting: conquer, pillage, rape,
like some grotesque dramatization
of imperial nightmares? Past is prologue…

Why write a poem when
the sky is falling, LA is burning,
and the foxes have been given
control of the hen house?

What can a poem
even do?

Can these poems
be a balm
for the fear settled over
us now like hot ashes,
re-igniting with each
news notification?
Can they cradle
the sorrow I experience
knowing that my neighbors
want this?
Can they hold
tender spaces - Can
joy skip with these words
as they play?
Can I cook you
some warm soup here?

What can a poem
even do?

GRIEF AND LONGING

Black Coffee and God

I want,
always…
      always want…
            more
than black coffee
and God,

This longing I fail
to erase lingers
on edges,
      badgers me
to hike trails,
follow pebbles
      I recognize
towards shadows,
and lick wounds,
certain there is
      magic beneath
or, at the very least --
      devastation,
      sugar cubes,
      and rich cream.

Ghosts

Intrepid specters
shadow my architecture,
remind me of sweaters
abandoned in closets
and beard butter resting
on porcelain whispering
blame, bird never in
hand, my tight
grip never enough,
or too much.

I free fall from nest,
futile and weak,
more kindling.
for fire, beat back
ghosts that
keep placing
blood on
my hands.

In rebellion, I rise
to rinse in river
gather new sticks,
green moss, and mud…
and begin again.

Gilded Carriage

You said I must be a witch but
it was you,
running your warm hands across my sternum,
pressing my small wrists between your thumbs,
that put a spell on me.

I thought you were a good decision.

Instead of guitar strings,
your fingers pressed computer keys.
Wrapped in wool sweaters, you smelled like
sandalwood and respectability,
with every drawer on your well-made dresser
gliding silently and smoothly into place.

Generosity cloaked the
hollow darkness
leaking through crevices in your
carefully crafted vessel.
We pretended not to see.

Oh, how willing I was
to trade in my hand-made shoes
for a room at the Ritz,
and all the oysters I could eat.

Lost Boy

How could I blame you
when you were only bones
tucked inside a flannel
beaten black and blue
by your own belt?

Wrists wrapped in
layers of
white gauze,
after failing
at the romance of
a finale in a
clawfoot tub.

I tucked you in
like one of my children
and spoke
to the angels on
your behalf,
convinced them
to grant you
another temporary
reprieve.

The Mean Reds

A switch flips,
and the terror compels
me to grasp
at
ghosts,
to chase cheap imitations,
and plead for poison to guzzle
as an antidote to this hollow,
demanding scream threatening
to engulf me in memories or hallucinations,
holding my head down,
forcing me to witness my bones
attempting to jump ship.

In the face of this
utter aloneness,
alien even to the aliens,
I grip the edge
of my well-worn
sanity, lift the
collar of my brown
peacoat, and wish to
smoke cigarettes.

I cry out to wild mother
instead, breathe in fire,
flip the switch again, and I see…

I am warm and I am fed and
I cannot recall what
all the fuss was about,
or why I was so
certain I would perish.

For All the People Who Died

Jim Carroll has already written this poem …

All about those brilliant, sensitive
types, prone to despair
and delusions, who were
delirious on love until
it crashed into jagged
cliffs bound to
impale hope and
slaughter ecstasy, who
created soundtracks with
moans of pleasure and
pain like free solo
climbing balanced on
edges, the possibility
of greatness or demise
on either side, until
one day it ended. And the
art never made hovers now
around me, asking if I might have
pulled them to safety
had I only had the right
words? And the charred
memories follow me
across desolate fields
like a soldier surviving
a senseless war.

Modern Tragedy

Swirls of muddy
drywall, like all
our pretty words,
masked cracks
in the foundation.
That tiny house,
a balloon
overfilled with
our daydreams…
precariously balanced
on hard work
and iron will,
trudging only for
modest heights,
and a little romance
but ill-fated
just the same.

Clenched teeth
whisper fights
over the head of
a toddler swinging
between us
hand in hand.
Public apologies
sung on stages extend
to heated therapy

between cool sheets.
Life/death/life
hawk circles like
musical chairs until
only one remains.

Astro

This bass reminds me of a shape I once took,
and this guitar of that time I believed you were magic.
Nostalgia intertwines with desire…
How many times have I stood in front of live wires...
The promise of intensity and rapture
rip thru my veins like the start of a speedball or the
first few meetings with a new lover.

After this winter of my heart, this tomb
I've cocooned in with your ashes.
Better to lie dormant,
to hibernate in this cave with a warm fire and
Netflix, Tommy Shelby's pain is romantic
when it isn't lying next to me
suffocating me with separation,
the heat from his body drifting across
a 6-inch uncrossable trench.

From inside this home built of bricks and boundaries
I watch more insanity arise.
Misogynistic bounties and the poor still buying lies -
weighing me down…

As much as
the weight from my hibernation,
the weight of my sorrow,
the weight of your glorious lives resting

in the palms of my hands.
These hands she calls pretty…
they used to play piano,
hold Marlboro reds, and
perfect pints of Jim Beam;
now they pay bills, and stir pastas,
and hold your fears and dreams.

I need to laugh again.
To feel vibrations of the living,
dance with possibilities and risk mistakes.
The breath of September on my neck
whispers in my ear,
Come and play…
It's time.

My Name in Your Mouth

My name in your mouth
a scolding,
sounds intimate like
playground days.
A warning
about high places
and hot stoves,
      I will not heed.

My name in your mouth
a whisper swallowed, unspoken,
a scream trapped
under a mountain
of obligation,
of costumes,
of whistles in the dark.
      I hear you anyway.

My name in your mouth
escapes through your eyes
enters the ends of my nerves
with vibration,
loudly calls me
like a siren,
      I resist.

My name in your mouth
like the bass in a funk band,
like the current in the river,
belongs there –
too natural, too powerful,
to be kept captive –
waiting for permission to sing.

Love me, Love me

I still hand over the reins
of my worth
            to odd characters
                        I imbue with a magic
I believe I lack.

Never are they
            the heroes I imagine,
like the outcasts in movies,
            steeped in bravery
                        and moral high ground,
loyal to the death.

Instead,
allegiance is conditional and
            shifting,
no one is drawing a sword
            to protect my honor,
and the one who must summon courage is
            always me.

Longing

Longing for a
human home
to crawl into,
the moon laps up
desires left on
spine, whispers
into clavicles,
and between ribs,
mixed tapes of
memories and
fantasies, mis-
guiding my brittle
arrows into hardwood
and dead trees.
Trace this longing
round my lips,
spread these ashes
over flames and
fields of poppies,
help me
carry a torch
for surprises.

Unmask

I scrape my knee
on layers of gravel
covered by pretty
gauze, play seek to
your hide under
taffeta and ties,
can't you still feel
the pea under all
those mattresses,
cause I sure can…

Let me loosen this
braided cord around
my rib, hand it
over, let you carry
the weight of your
own discoveries,
I have enough
madness of my
own to unpack,
and besides, what if
I pull free this brick and
find it was the keystone
to your solid, pretty arch?

See Saws and Hand Grenades

I am compelled to attach myself
to impossible things…
see saws and hand grenades…
Pull the pin,
and see where the damage lands.

Curiosity killed the cat,
they say…
It's taken me to some interesting places.
(Or at least, places that appeared so
before they revealed themselves.)
A record on repeat…
A dazzling ouroboros
devouring its tail
with full conviction
it's capturing something new,
until the déjà vu
says I've seen this picture
before, rolled this boulder
up this same mountain
last year;
didn't make it that time,
neither.

New faces shine
on pedestals built from
old wounds,
seeking belonging,

seeking a wolf pack
to curl up with and
be cleaned,
be made worthy.

Hoping to catch
aloofness, to
roll up late,
and not fear death.

Turns out –
a Sanga
is less warm bath
and more
hall of mirrors.

PLAY

When Burying Your Wedding Dress

When burying your wedding dress,
make sure to cloak it in
a large box,
inside a dark trash bag,
so the waste management
workers whisk it away
without seeing it
and feeling sorry for you,
or worse yet, thinking your
a privileged bitch
who discards expensive
things instead of recycling them.

When burying your wedding dress
remember you aren't really
discarding magic,
just the naive faith that
the gorgeous silver stitching
could hold a marriage together
when it ripped at the seams.

When burying your wedding dress,
worry less about disappointing the crowd,
and more about gathering
treasures for your new
apartment.

Go on a hunt for the pieces of you
that have been in hiding.
Try watching elephants in Chiang Mai
or the Northern Lights in Anchorage.
Sign up for a retreat,
or run a marathon.

When burying your wedding dress,
let a pound of pebbles go with it.
Let it be final.
Smile and wave.

Pretty Boys

Lips on the back of
my tired neck.
Warm hands on
weary shoulders.
Hips against hips.
I melt into pleasure,
and it is
delicious.

And yet,
I must remember –
He is particle board,
not oak.
Don't lean too hard;
he won't hold.

This is role play –
where he is strong,
and I am soft –
the opposite of truth.
My vanity still
wants a pretty face,
enthusiasm,
without the weight

But some days, I wonder –
what inner work must I do
to change my kink
to inner fortitude, and
Is there an app for that?

Ethical non-monogamy - 3 Haikus

Three lovers delight…
My mom's funeral, alone,
Meet for brunch after.

Your wife accepts this,
I get the fun parts of you,
You shovel her snow.

When I get cancer,
girlfriends drive me to chemo,
you are free to go.

Boredom

This boredom,
I do not tolerate
well; give me
fire to walk thru or
a prize chicken
to celebrate;
Let me pull
a sword from my
thigh, declare
my love on a rooftop, or
dance down the street
praising a saint.

Or, I might just kick up
sorrow buried beneath
dust, create stories
of imagined injury, or
crack open a door that
should remain closed,
just to lend an arc to
the season, to keep
up my interest
in this incarnation.

Ungraceful

I am meant to
age gracefully
and smart like
Diane Keaton,
but here I am
instead, finding myself
more of the Dylan Thomas
variety, hurling rage
at symbols, or looking
for loopholes ala
Dorian Grey, where is
my magic painting? What
must I lock inside the attic
to stay pretty forever?
Damn the consequences,
come what may! I am
loathe to let go of
yesterday's toys; tell me,
if I keep you
in my bed, will your illusions
seep through my skin,
make me believe again?
In truth, I lack
the humility to be
supporting cast,
new adventures call, and I
crave at least one more
grand romance.
It seems terribly dull to quietly
fade to black, and I suddenly
understand old ladies
in eccentric purple hats.

Ode to Cigarettes

Oh cigarettes, appendage of
my intellect, a weighted
blanket for my anger and
anxiety, a muzzle for my
tongue, how I mourn you,
upon awakening, after
a good meal, post-coital,
or alongside of 24-hour
diner coffee and deep analysis
with a like-minded friend.

How I miss
the nonchalance you
gifted me, the ability
to wash the workday away,
all of my give-a-fucks
fading with each puff,
as you decorated my disillusionment
with a casual shrug.

I miss the pause you
could lend to a heated
argument with a partner,
muting the emotion
just enough to return to
denial and find a band-aid
that would stop the
hemorrhaging for at least
a few more weeks.

Or the way you offered
me five minutes

alone on the porch, while
I watched the kids play
legos through the
picture window and
slipped into daydreams

I miss the way you
led me to my people,
huddled in solidarity outside
funerals and baby showers,
free to disconnect from
what was happening inside,
the rituals of a society we
didn't quite belong to.

Or, how having you in hand
sometimes held me in place
for just one more minute, kept
me from bolting, while a
plan formulated, or new
idea emerged, or a friend
called to remind me
I am not alone.

My Potential

Gifted and talented...Gifted and talented...
They talked about my potential
Put me in that mixed grade class
where we learned calligraphy
and focused on inquiry-based learning
because it would be more "authentic"

Authentic...
What I authentically wanted to
inquire about at age 10 was
how to be as cool as
Vicky Marsiglio with her black bra
and her swinging hips
or as tough as that greasy haired boy
who jumped off the top of the
jungle gym at Friday's recess
and sliced his hand wide open
while we all watched in admiration.

Gifted and talented
My potential chased me,
made me take tests that
qualified me for scholarships
to pricey private schools
I had no interest in attending.
I ran backwards
to stay a part of
the crowd,

pretended not to know answers
I knew. Who wants to be a smart girl,
when you could ride in the
passenger seat of Pete Alexopoulos's
Black Mustang instead?

You have to choose, you know.

Gifted and talented
They invited me to join the
National Honors Society.
My mother found the letter crumpled
in the bottom of my backpack,
hidden and discarded like
my potential.

Despite aiming for average,
Kalamazoo College,
recognized my potential -
gave me a scholarship
to walk their classic quad
I read all the great
philosophers,
memorized the history
of art painted on cave walls,
and smoked weed while listening
to Ani Difranco and

debating alternatives to capitalism.
Tired of listening to me talk,
my college roommate pushed me
to protest,
to join her in action
to fulfill my potential.
I resisted,
quit school instead,
ran backwards
into dark bar rooms
where I could numb
the thoughts and
feelings of
my gifted and talented brain.

Ironic then, that now,
I wonder why these mediocre
white men who lack vision
are in charge of everything,
failing to lead in the ways
I think they should.

Where I rejected ambition,
they've embraced it;
Where I've avoided
stepping into power
I feel won't fit,
they've slipped it on
with full confidence that

this coat was meant to suit their frame.
The responsibilities I fret over balancing,
They simply outsource guilt-free to dutiful wives.
Their audacity has outpaced their potential
While my potential's been pacing the floor.

Gifted and talented
Gifted and talented
It is true what they say…
There is no payout for potential.

WAILING

Wailing

The preacher asked the family
to place hands on her
and then gave her permission to
wail.

So, she wailed for her mother
not to leave her, to return
like Lazurus
in time for her prom send off
and to witness her walk the stage at
graduation…
As she expelled agony
from her spirit,
it found a landing place in
us, mingled with our own
losses, lifted band aids
from ancient wounds,
and soaked the large congregation
in their own tears
suddenly freed from captivity.

We wept
We….
Wept, a powerful collective
weeping, and I knew then
that we could all use
more wailing.

We walk through loss,
after loss like warriors,
keep it moving –
put your grief in a box
to take out at night
to cradle
when you're alone
so no one has to deal
with your sad face.

Daily we watch kids die
at the hands of police in the city,
or at the hands of soldiers in Gaza,
or at the hands of their classmates
in a school meant to be safe.

We feel it gather
in our bellies,
consume our hearts
and crawl up our esophagus.
Then we take sip of coffee,
swallow the wail and
get ready for work.

But I am convinced
if we don't expel this scream,
it will cripple us;
it will transform into
knots and ulcers

and cysts and cancers.
I've lost whole body parts
from holding onto
shit, when I needed to
let go
and
wail.

But I was reminded by this Baptist preacher
on a Sunday afternoon,
in a Mack Avenue church,
that we need not wail alone,
in secret,
where we won't disturb others.
He said, "Sister, let it all out…You are loved.
We are here."
We wept as she wailed.

We must give each other permission,
parallel play our grief,
scream next to our neighbor,
or be a steady light post
in the face of another's wail,
until we digest, metabolize,
shed enough layers
to uncover the place in us
that still wants to sing.

Wild Tongue

Why did I spend so much time
wrestling this wild tongue
into a button up
with a necktie
when howling naked at the moon
was calling me?

I might have set the house on fire
like Left Eye,
but I choked...
on suggestions,
and rightness, and rules;
a spiritual grave of goodness
burying the wolf under
layers of language
and lipstick…

My organs boiling
as I chewed gum
and spoke love
and listened to
the people
praise me.

Election Season

I let you come inside...
your blue eyed,
piercing hard body
stamped me
VALID,
a shallow pool
I mistook for harmless...

But now?
Now,
I am drowning,
and finally, I see clearly
as you cast your ballot,
as you vote for
my destruction,
that you favor me beneath you
In more places than the bedroom

And You?
You
are the enemy
within.

Revolution and Sugarcane

The Elephants will do anything
                      for sugarcane.

The young people are calling
for revolution (on both sides).
I went to a shooting range
to prepare, picked up
a revolver for the first time ever,
and expelled my anger
into the silhouette of a man.

My rage feels collective,
covers things I haven't
experienced held quietly in DNA
with shame, never allowed
to escape painted lips,
passed down for me
to wrestle onto the page --
10,000 screams
buried in baked goods
and loads of laundry.
Iron and drink.
Iron and drink.

But now, I have a gun in my hand
instead of a pen, preparing for
the revolution, and I will still do anything
for sugarcane.

Canary (For Luigi)

This glee that folks
be expressing though,
a canary in the
coalmine of for-profit
healthcare and corporate
controlled government;
an avatar for our
collective powerlessness;
a beacon of hope that
we might stop blaming immigrants,
or our struggling neighbors,
and start directing
our wrath at those
who build empires
off our labor and
our dis-ease.

A fatal warning shot to
remind them of what
little people will do
when you don't re-distribute
enough to keep them satisfied,
and the pain overthrows
the apathy, but the devils
coming in are the cocky kind
that don't know history
or heed signs...
So, they only see
a yellow bird,
easily captured and alone.

A glutinous,
old boys club
that will never atone.
When we can't afford bread,
and we have no recourse,
is there still power in the pen?
or only the sword?

I Forgive You (and then I unforgive)

I forgive you,
and then I unforgive…
You pulverized my
pictures of you,
now just a pile of dust,
once a collage of your best
role play; a mirage I was
desperate to see.

I forgive you
and then I unforgive…
You only shattered
this solid frame because your
own spirit had been
splintered by cruel figures of
power pretending
to be heroes, so you
lit love like a sparkler,
then held it an
arm's width away.
And you didn't
have the courage
to speak truth in love
so you played the
Wizard of Oz instead.

I forgive you
and then I unforgive…
You were just a babe
in a grown man's coat,

shook and shell-shocked
that the money couldn't fix it,
that all the inner work hadn't fixed it,
that I could see behind the curtain,
that here you were,
frozen – the same.

I forgive you
and then I unforgive,
and the rage
ripples through me
again.

BEARING WITNESS

Twinkling

In this space
for the hope-mongers
shouting possibilities,
in these unlikely circles
of the risen dead.

I watch delight spring
free as stones are lifted,
a reverse Salem pressing,
Slowly, then, all at once,
a twinkling discovered
beneath it all.

Your playfulness
lifts grief's lingering
gauze from my frame,
untangles laughter, recalls
girlhood, recalls
lightness like lemonade
shared with skater boys
on front porch in a
sweltering summer
after 7th grade.

I desire to tangle
my fingers through your aura
and wrap limbs around limbs,

to curl up in your flannel,
bask under your spotlight,
and taste the joy in connection --
to be present, embodied, and free.

And to deny
any consequence
for such visceral callings,
for such generous
gifts to spirit.

High School

Irreverent laughter
travels in packs,
lifts stale tablecloths,
revealing warped wood.
Scent of cheap
cologne drifts
off cocky heads
nodding,
initiated hands clasp
in complex dances,
speaking recognition.

Round stain revealed
left by an abandoned
glass of apple juice
turned into potent wine.
Shoulder comes up
against shoulder
reassurance he
won't disappear;
he is real,
like you
      are
          real

Listen to the lady,
she has some
thing you want,
maybe…maybe keys
to the cabinet with the
tablecloths…

For Ocean Vuong

You crawl up
into my heart
and turn dials,
tuning my aorta
until I feel
       you
          absorbing
war and excavation
of hearts aching, and
working it out
against stubble and
tender muscle, an unlikely
refuge I recognize
how jigsaw
pieces can fit
unexpectedly and
gift solace like
CPR, jumpstarting
breath in a
body just
drowning.

My Favorite Song

My favorite song is
whispers and giggles
through closed bedroom doors,
where you trade tales of
crushes, or mischief, or
wistful daydreams. My heart
expands gladl, so much better
than the times when it was sobs
drifting my way at 3 am
that stretched it.

I crawled into your bed
to cradle you on
those sleepless nights,
so powerless to bring comfort,
or fix what had been broken….
a mere mortal woman,
with no magic
save forehead kisses and pasta.

My heart grew in those days too,
ached with the grandeur of
grief and inadequacies,
But today, it swells with honor,
to be a humble witness to
these two young women
becoming.

Delia

Her laughter is a new edition,
erupting in small uncertain bursts
from around a hand ready
to stuff it back
in quickly and
smother it with a swallow.

This is a change, from last
year's silence,
sitting back to wall,
talking only in
bite size whispers
to boy who smelled
the burning and believed
he could put out the fire
with his charm.

She is leaving class
every Thursday now
for counseling,
has recently
began testifying
against stepdad.
The only time she tears up
is when she tells me
how he used to string her
dog up downstairs and whip him

while she listened.
She can cry for this
cruelty; It's somehow safer
than crying for what he did to her.

Breath is possible now
with the secrecy lifted.
A sentence commuted
Space expands
and she fills it –
tentative
like a toddler
taking first steps,
Girlfriends hold out
hands, envelop her,
become protective mothers,
as she finds solid footing,
and takes flight.

For Marianne Faithful

So long, Marianne,
patron saint of female
heroin addicts and
women who never
got as much recognition
for their art as they
got for being the girlfriend
of So and So. So long,
Marianne, resilient icon
of style and bravery.
Sister of morphine and
cigarettes and girls
who can't get no satisfaction
from men or motherhood,
or the freedom promised
by the street,
emerging ravaged
and wonderful,
throat pouring out
gravel gifts
for us to crawl into
and feel seen.

On The Road

Your hand caresses shaved hair
at the base of your neck
flashing soft skin of under arm
thin like underbelly of fish,
light as flash paper,
revealing fragility masked
by the wide expanse of upper back
and the purposeful set of your jaw.

Pendulum swings
king to pauper.
You light up the stage,
a god of swagger and fire,
A hollow prize followed by
hotel rooms crowded
with silence, questions hanging
in the corners like cobwebs.
mistaking lyrics
for answers,
for wisdom,
for love.

A chameleon succeeding
in the present,
but always stuck
one step behind…

A waitress wears her smile;
A laugh at the bar
brings you back to Toronto.
The way his brown hair curls
at the base of his neck lingers
at the edge of your awareness,
a peripheral memory
to return to
when the train brakes
and you can catch your breath.

Until then,
applause smothers longing,
and sunglasses dim regret.

Carlos

Part I

You looked so Detroit
that day at the Metropark
in your heavy black Dickies outfit
buttoned only at the top,
revealing white tank underneath
and chain wallet secured at your hip.
Your black hair falling
thick and damp
over hooded eyes.

There would be no frolicking
in sunlight for you,
no splashing in wave pools
or spiking volleyballs
across nets.
A class picnic does not
have the power to change
your shape,
to alter this calculated
hardness
and reveal boyhood.

The heat from late May sun
eventually pushed you
to discard a layer
and by afternoon

I caught a moment
of joy
escaping your lips,
despite your best
efforts to wrestle
it into a sardonic grin.

Part II

With my own system calibrated
to codependency,
the hairs on my neck
knew there was a problem
before the other teachers,
who were oblivious to
the precariousness
of that momentary lapse into
lightness.

Phone to ear,
I saw you at a distance
pacing like a tiger
trapped behind glass.
I approached with caution
to find tears streaming
freely down damp cheeks.
"I have to go." you informed me
with a fierceness I did not question.
Child gone in an instant,
adult in its place

"My daughter is in the hospital."

You started to walk.
It was 40 miles back to the city,
but you'd feel less powerless
if you were moving.

I caught up with you
drove you back to school,
reassuring you,
parent to parent now,
that your baby would
survive her fever
and thrive.

"Thank you, Miss"
You step out of my car into yours
replacing tears
with the mask of man,
of dad, of silent strength.
Ready to walk into
the hospital with words
of faith.

Part III

I hear your street name
in student chatter
before I get the email.
I ask, and they answer.

Carlos and his brother
shot by rival gang members
on Springwell on Sunday.
Two sons, two fathers
gone. A funeral
full of women
carrying the pain
wrought by men,
carrying on
for the children,
carrying the hope
they can protect
the next generation
from repeating this cycle.

Carlos's daughter bouncing
on the chair next to her mother
in a pretty pink dress,
hair expertly woven into black braids,
too young to know
the sharp turn her life just took.
Violence wrought upon her
by those who never even saw her.

Part IV

What I remember:

Carlos hated Holden Caulfield,
thought he was a whiny bitch.
He loved his baby girl.
He couldn't yet commit.
Torn between a brotherhood
and dreams of a future he
couldn't
quite
see.

Sometimes being on the fence
is a dangerous place to be.

Peace

1000 deep lines
criss cross your face,
each crease a page
of your story rich
and full of neighborhood
hide and seek,
siblings more plentiful
than fingers that held
jacks and marbles
and dreamt of
playing the piano.

Each fold
a tapestry of tales...
unexpected romance
and babies
blooming in gardens
of daffodils and
brown-eyed Susans,
yellow like the sunshine
you bring to rooms
even when endings
bring sorrow, and sickness
claims power over sister's
mind full of memories
slipping now
like water down drains,
fading like the sound

of ice cream trucks
you could never catch
on hot summer days.
Your smile deepens
this road map
of survival and joy
that I hold on to.
Your beauty, present
and unshakeable,
shines.

Crone years beckon me,
and I am unafraid.

PLACE

Michigan

Dreaming of feet padding soft dirt,
mindfully stepping over thick,
determined roots, fingertips
caressing stones collected in pockets,
smell of pine carrying peace
with the breeze, birds singing
so high I cannot find them,
crunch of sticks revealing
a white tail deer who locks
eyes for an intimate moment,
before gracefully retreating
deeper into forest I am
getting lost in,
time stopping,
pressure to produce .
disappearing as breath
recalibrates connection to trees.
Mother earth kissing skin,
speaking softly –
All is well.
All is well.
You belong here.

The Schvitz

Deep emerald leather and dark wood wainscoting
suggest luxuries beyond my east side expectations
American Spirit smoke floats on heady words
mapping potential playmates and career daydreams

In a space once barred to us, we laugh --
we laugh the grand belly howls of the liberated.
We feast on rich rare steak and don't worry about
who listens as we tell tales of conquests and defeats.

We, who are so very alive,
Alive, when so many like us haven't made it,
We descend the stairs to sit on benches of cedar,
embracing rising steam off recently drenched coals.

Limbs softening as our sweat releases
the resin of stories still trapped in our fascia;
grief and old beliefs pour off our forms and
clear space for something new;
An icy womb awaits to anoint us
with a holy and heart racing
rebirth – if we can brave the leap.

As expansive, and as big, as we want to be.
Joyously and wholly human,
in community, and embraced.
In this old Detroit underground
ceramic tiled banya,
A woman and free.

Bishop Street

This house
smells like firewood and
freedom; reminds me of the year
I reclaimed my soul
from the pinched face,
bleach blonde, mean-girl
boaters, who love America
and hate immigrants except
for their Nona, who can't understand
why all lives don't matter, and
why people can't keep their sexualities
and their politics to themselves.

From the men who need
constant forgiving,
who paint pictures of
themselves as Mount Rushmore
when in fact they are like
the ashes in my fireplace
or a dry sandcastle on a windy day.

From the well-meaning folk
who just want to see me
married because they want me to
"have people," and by people
they mean a man
who will notice
if I don't come home at night.

From three prepared meals
at the kitchen table
and perfectly manicured lawn expectations.
From never missing a day
of work or school unless
you're throwing up, and from being
agreeable to bosses and teachers
no matter what.

That year I stopped shrinking my shine
to make others more comfortable,
stopped wrapping my anger up
in pretty little boxes
with presentable bows.

Released,
I followed the beacon
where it led
into my soul,
and into new spaces
with hearts like mine,
and into this old Detroit house
made of red bricks and hardwood
with the big oak tree out back
that sheds acorns
like I'm shedding stories
So fresh growth may emerge.

Ancient Oak

This massive and ancient oak
speaks to me, whispers answers to
questions I haven't asked
tangled beneath
deep soil, like her roots
winding silently under
earth creating tripping
hazards too easily overlooked.

She reminds me --
Do nothing.
Rock yourself in a hammock,
listen to the starlings' protest,
the cardinals sing
their gospel of hope,
and the wind introducing
herself to the leaves.
Let goddess hold you
in palm of her hand,
like this hammock.

Feel your roots, sturdy
with experience of ancestors,
and the nourishment of
years of rain. When it is time,
the path will be clear.

Detroit Winter

Bleak December
bleeds the
last shreds of
my well-played
optimism,
disintegrates into
sewer steam
rising to cloak my
naked loneliness
buried deep inside
my puffy coat.

Icy shadows
stalk,
hound my
footsteps
marking time
on damp
city streets,
cackle
in recognition.

Cold Cold Full Moon

The Cold Full Moon
of December
ushers me toward
the Solstice.
The longest
and the darkest night
of this frigid winter
seems brighter
because my soul
shed 7 layers of soot
and carnage this year,
uncovered pleasure and play,
traded in shame
for celebration,
truth, and liberation.

Allow the dark to temper,
make tender,
this vessel, hear my
hopes scratched
onto sticky notes
and dropped into
fireplace flames,
Detroit's version of the
wailing wall; wrap me in
this blanket of llama wool,
as the yule log burns,
bringing blessings
abundant.

Snowfall in a Winter of Fires

And then one marvelous evening,
snow finally falls,

a weighted blanket for my
spirit, weary and worn
from trying to outpace
monsters like
self-recrimination,
rejection,
and time.

I surrender to rest
and re-
member,
to just be.

Spring

The determined crocus
forces her head through
the icy ground,
past the dry, stubborn
stalks of fall.

Here I am!
Tada!

My magic is real;
believe in yours.
Allow breastbone to splinter;
light will pour through.

Here I am!
Tada!

Spirit not snuffed out
after all.
Another season
of nonsensical,
irrepressible
hope.

Absurdly,
against all reason,
we leap one more time.

for the alternative
is the long swim,
the numbness of a spoon,
or the boredom
intolerable.

Tiny flame flickers
ignites imagination,
busts through the frozen
landscape,
looking for adventure
like the
purple crocus in
a Detroit Spring.

Here I am!
Tada!

Manresa

What a luxury,
for a woman
to retreat from giving
into a room of my own,
with a twin bed and a desk,
a sacred space to let these thoughts
run out on paper into the
Be-Still-And-Know-I-Am air.

The roof out my window -- alive
with shingles that shimmer
hues of violet and blue,
like the generous Rainbow Fish,
patron saint of sharing
in children's storybooks.
It's giving
fairytale cottage,
or the hermitage
of a wise old man in folklore.

How many seekers
have sat at this desk
spilling fears and prayers out of pens,
walked these grounds listening
for God to whisper answers for
stubborn scar tissue,
or pled with Mary at her grotto
for some balm to heal festering wounds?

What if the Rainbow Fish
changed her mind?
can she get the scales back -
bring back her shine?

Jesus suffers on crosses
in every direction here
reminding me
I am not alone,
my crosses are quite bearable,
and even he fell three times.

I got to see you in my dreams last night;
memories bubble, demand attention,
pain asking to be heard and felt.
The talk is on forgiveness --
I'm willing in both directions.
Just etch-a-sketch the whole mess,
We were kids;
we knew not what we did.

Can I breathe free now?
Can I stop looking for my salvation
in gods with skin?
Let this holy water
make me holy
whole again,
Amen.

Mt. LeConte in April

Balancing on black slate,
I breathe in mountain
trees, heart racing as
calves take on inclines,
steep and jagged. I
concentrate, purposefully
place each foot; a fall
could be fatal, but the air
soothes worry and we know
we've conquered worse.

We are warriors, after all,
intimate with pain;
our burning quads,
a paltry symbol
for the fire of sorrow,
of passion, of rage,
we've walked
hand in hand with
for miles, for months,
for years – this trek,
we can endure.

Finally,
the peak juts out
jagged and fierce,
overlooking sprawling,
blue-green trees, as
endless as the
cotton candy sky
throwing a party for
our triumph. We try

to carry it home
in photos, but
the feeling resists
capture. My heart
expands, and for an
ephemeral moment,
my breath becomes
God.

Time Flies Here

Like sands through the hourglass,
the days of our lives be slipping by,
with teen angst and clove
cigarettes melting into
into Fender Strat magic,
mescaline, and love,
that would later drown
under the weight of
10,000 needles,
and absolute need
chasing me out of town.
Shifts into meetings
drenched in black coffee
and 12 step voodoo,
and a tattooed
dream boy with
a Murphy bed.

Soon we're gazing
in awe at our baby girl
in her Raggedy Ann crib, and
I'm walking down an aisle
in a white dress, moving
furniture into brightly colored
bungalow, student teaching,
new baby on the way;
You are playing music again;
we are not smoking;

Until floor drops, and I
hold a Camel while
packing my car with all
the belongings I can fit
and our two girls,
sprinting for shelter
from your addiction,
dodging landmines
and holding my breath.

Looking for God
In 3 am terror and
unity churches and
Buddhist temples,
Finding life on yoga
mats and in meditation.
Carried to a tiny new house,
evolving from a we to an I.
I, as in I parent alone, as their
baby steps, turn into missing teeth,
turn into bikes and roller skates,
first kisses, and heartbreaks.

Men come and go with seasons,
until one stays for some years,
keeps me on a pretty pedestal
with promises that evaporate,
and now tattooed dream boy,
turned father, and husband,
turned ex, and finally friend,
dies alone in a hotel room,
and I exhale because the worst
has happened and we are all
still here.

Enter a pandemic forcing us
to stop and puzzle; We write
as if our lives depend on it
because they do.

I buy a house in Detroit,
as daughter goes to college
and finishes in the blink
of a cat's eye,
and I find myself
sitting inside my dreams
in cafes in strange countries,
practicing presence while
climbing mountains.

I cannot capture these foreign
sunsets like I can
writing words for
academia so they let me
back in, with hopes that
maybe I can get
something of value
on record before
it's all over.
Sand is flowing
again.

313

Ode to this city that
raised me, broadened
my imagination, inspired
creation, taught me
about Black and Mild's,
P-Funk, and Falafel,
brought me to ecstasy
and my own depravity;
my heart tethered
to layers of memories
knitted into the fabric
before my time -- scar battled
and full of stubborn pride; My
old Detroit is new to
Old Detroiters;

My Old Detroit held
heroes in Doc Martens
with heads nodding to
punk rock played in
underground afterhours
joints, kids sitting on
stoops outside Zoots holding
Colt 45 or Mad Dog in brown
paper bags, Larry perpetually
wielding drumsticks
on corners, riffing about politics

and the Beatles, and old Tyrone
slinging his one arm around me, saying
one of these days, sister,
lending me money for
the payphone to call the man,
cause we all need a hand sometimes.
On this corner, where the
Red Door and Revolution Books
once danced, where I passed
balloons in dark rooms, and
learned about Plato and Marx from
old communists with grey goatees,
now stands a brightly lit cafe,
a pricey retail shop, and hot yoga;
Like a censored record, this corner
wiped clean of expletives and grit.

But new Detroit blood still
pumps art through
these streets as folks breathe
life on to city walls, celebrating
larger-than-life Detroit
beauty. And even in
new Detroit, bullets
litter neighborhoods
with tears, while hope flies
with children, and poetry,
and music at open mics;

Gears grind at assembly plants,
and in the minds of
ambitious young people
hustling in community,
building new potentialities
with vegan food trucks,
garden record parties,
and emo rap filled with language
of hearts healing. Energy
moving away from insulation
and towards connection
and expansion. New Detroit
calling old Detroit in.

Playas del Coco

The best thing
about a cafe
in a foreign land,
is that it is exquisitely
just a café; it holds
no memories,
no history,
none of my stories
live here; ghosts aren't
hovering, nor current
duties or desires; the bird calls
don't carry your voice,
the flyers on the wall,
are for bands I do not
recognize, the conversation
at the table next to me easily
tuned out in a language
not my own, the
Me of Detroit,
a distant impression, less etched
in stone. My dramas
revealed as play acting
out chosen roles. Am I
more me, or less me,
with no past and no
attachments? I do not
know, but my heart
here,
feels free,
a fresh slate,
an unknown.

New Moon

Let this new moon
give birth
      to contentment;
seeds buried under
layers of snow and
clay, hard and frozen,
rest peacefully now,
all resistance finally faded;
the energy spent
chasing sunlight has left;
there is warmth here,
if I can only remember to look.

CELEBRATIONS

Pilgrims and Poets

I belong to the pilgrims and the poets,
seekers of the words and the Way.
Some of them fell off the earth
searching for Truth;

They looked for
a road map on the faces of elders,
and saw only judgment.

Still,
they found God in the blisters
on the souls of their feet,
and sitting criss-cross in the valley of divinity,
they cracked-open with child-like awe.

On those mornings,
joy erupted,
illuminating anyone
lucky enough to be near.

Other days they couldn't
recall with sufficient force
that it existed,
and got sidetracked following despair,
mistaking it for wisdom.

I belong to the pilgrims and the poets.

If they had been able
to slay their mother,
swaddle their dragons,
and metabolize their pain,
they might be here
with me
still.

I wish to go to the desert
or an Ashram,
to meditate on a mountain top,
to follow the pilgrimage
of the Incas,
or walk El Camino de Santiago,

but the road keeps leading
to the dark forest within.
I am excavating my spirit
for gems,
and tossing out
fool's gold.

Some Men

Some men are of earth,
smell of damp clay
molded like mountains
cradling wildflowers,
dew gathers at
nape of neck as they
make you breakfast,
fire smolders under
breastbone, visible
in pupils and felt
in calloused palms
warming your skin,
rough, tender
touch carrying
Quan Yin, but also
Kali; if you can
surrender to this
alchemy, you will
transform before
he returns to dust.

Tucked Away

Sometimes I walk into a place and before
I can gather a defense,
my breath is ripped from me,
and I tumble into a time-space vortex

The smell, or the lights, or the music,
or some artwork on the wall
suddenly attacks me with memories
of places like this
and people I was
or people I am still
in another dimension
or on another timeline
in a parallel universe

Longing fills my lungs and
threatens to choke me
with the possibilities I skipped,
and the chances I blew,
and I desperately miss,
the person I could be,
if I weren't this person that I am today

This person that I am today
who I love very dearly,
in an instant seems a flimsy cloak
with dozens of others lying dormant beneath the surface

And I wish to be more people,
to have more lives,
to be able to consciously exists on multiple timelines,
playing it all the different ways I could play it

No matter how much I write,
I cannot empty all these stories;
No matter how much I wrestle with the words,
I cannot ever capture correctly
that place, that time,
those people.

Whether it's the Sicilians playing pinochle
around my grandmother's kitchen table,
Or the K college hippies smoking hashish and planning revolution,
Or the creative geniuses playing funk and spinning stories,
at the blue warehouse in 1993,
Or the tragically hip gathered in Al's cramped room,
certain things would change on Monday,
Or the Vietnam vets at the Huntington hotel,
on a bleak Detroit December at 3 am,
Or the warm women's gatherings,
that wrapped up my rawness in a base layer I could build on.
Or that Day at the beach, when my babies were still babies, and
you were still alive.

I try to place this current wave of familiarity hitting me
in a coffee shop, in this city I've never been to,

and I settle on Kalamazoo, before deciding no --
it is a much earlier coffee den of my youth,
where I learned to chain smoke cigarettes
and appreciate beat poetry
read by pale boys with dark rimmed glasses,
and I wonder how Katie's doing,
and whatever happened to Dave Montgomery,
and to that guy that made art films and put me in one once

"Mom!"
I jump.
My daughter's voice pulls me out of my reverie.
Be here now. Be here now. I tell myself.

How many more layers can I add to this body? To these bones?
I wonder. How expansive is this soul?

Some moments I fear I will burst.

But just as often, I think --
there's so much yet to experience,
with not enough years left,
and I pray reincarnation is real,
and I get to have another go of it.

Sobriety – Year 25

I no longer stand in desperate lines
with my broken-backed
brethren cloaked in grimy
cardigans, shaking and
itching for the chance
to face a nurse in purple scrubs,
who avoids eye contact
and holds the serum to
reconnect my tissue
in her hands.

Not once in this millennium
have I waited "20 minutes"
for the man for three hours, or puked bile
at a gas station, surrendered family jewelry or
my boyfriend's guitar at a pawn shop,
had an abscess, stolen from a loved one,
or been barred from anyone's home

I haven't had to voluntarily
commit myself to a place
that tells me when to
get up in the morning, what chores to do,
who I can talk to, when it's lights out,
what meds I must take, or
who will be my accountability partner.

Instead,
I am free to roam these
rivers and roads, connect with
folks who are here today with me,
with the surreal awareness that
this moment is precious, for they
may all be gone tomorrow.
I am free to experience art
capturing the way
it all takes your breath away –
the joy and the rage.
I am free to wail in sorrow
for my lost comrades,
and to celebrate the
unlikely miracle
that I am still alive.

Soul Contracts

When I see you, I
see a puzzle piece
lost many moons
ago, your hues match
my soft tissue and
these tendons running
thru my frame like
monkey bars; your shape
gifts me optimism,
when I am partial to
despair.
Do you recognize me?
Do you sense
the portraits waiting for
our collaboration?
If I shout in celebration
like a toddler that
you have arrived, will you
meet me in a
grand embrace, or
lower seven veils
to avoid being seen?

Friends with my Face

Long gone are the days
when I wished
for thicker lips
and a smaller nose,
or pale skin like
Robert Smith,
so I could be
properly goth.

I have finally
made friends with my face --
The man in the glass,
as my father likes to say.

Somewhere between
West Genesee and Woodward,
alongside abandonment and rejection,
while kicking and screaming,
I was uncovering
that little one in the
yellow terry cloth jumper,
with the black braids,
shouting about winning
a ribbon for tying her shoes.

Falling for someone else
is much harder
these days,
now that I can discern
the difference between
oxytocin
and
love.

Butterflies and admiration
don't always come
hand in hand.

But I am friends with my face
these days, and
that makes
all the difference.

The Steppenwolf

Forever the Steppenwolf,
just a smidge removed…
Once chemically reinforced,
this distance now a habit,
both a blessing,
and a curse. Longing to
belong coerces me
into shapes I think will please;
but today or tomorrow
or next week, the cloak will drop,
my stripes will be revealed,
my spikes will poke through,
and then, I will remember –
I am a criatura salvaje
who cannot pretend,
who cannot survive
in shallow pools,
comfortably wrapped
in lukewarm lullabies,
whistling in the dark.
I must retreat to the
hermitage I built,
embrace my pacing
shadow screaming
"Bullshit!", give her a cookie
and acknowledge Truth.
Else, she will rip my soul
to shreds and push me off a cliff.

Freedom

I will no longer repent
for keeping a
secret trinket
just for me.

I will not sacrifice
everything on the
altar of intimacy,
or mistake a bit of joy
for the illusion of security.

I will favor my version,
put on my mask first,
and always keep
a secret trinket
just for me,

and I will not repent, and
I will not feel guilty.

Meditation

Your fingertips fold
me into soft
earth molded
shapes like
Klimt envisioned,
glittering gold,
steam rising,
the pressure cooker
of desire building
under your thumb
on my throat;

Palms cup
curves
on display,
your gaze --
oxygen
to my flame.
I follow my
breath to the exquisite,
fleeting moment
of no thought…

This is meditation…
better than the morning cold plunge,
or monastic denial,

embodied bodies in play,
pull me present
as they intertwine;
What a glorious gift…
a quiet mind.

The Green Light

Like Gatsby,
he still believed in
the green light,
and I didn't want
to be the one
to ruin it for him.
So I smiled sweetly,
cradled hope with him
that for sure, one day,
he would arrive.

I didn't have the heart
to tell him,
there is only now;
that when you get to that
dock across the bay,
she'll be gone,
or she'll be different,
or you'll be different;
one way or another,
the green light will move,
and you won't be there yet.

And when you think you glimpse
it again, on a mountain top,
you'll give chase,

put in miles of steps
to reach the peak,
only to find
the light has moved to the valley.

And the only real reason
to climb is if there is joy
in the climbing, and if you
are here with me now,
it is solely because
there is joy
in the dance.

Are You Taking Requests?

Can I request to sit cross legged at your feet
while you bellow songs of rage and
sorrow unleashed?

Can I lie beside you on my back
on your hardwood floor,
feel the vibration of my spine,
as you pluck strings
and sing sweet melodies –
as you call out to the Gods?

Can you tell them I am angry,
and I am grateful, and this hurts?

Can we trade these songs for
love? For proof of worth?

The Things Women Carry

Women carry things, like
lotions and lipsticks,
and pens in purses…
things like aspirin, and band aids,
and notepads in bags.

Women learn to carry secrets
like the blood between their legs,
like passing crushes at lockers
and stolen glances in Algebra…
Solve for x when x = just sexy enough
and y = too much of a slut.

Women carry resentments
by association for friends,
fiercely loyal, ready to defend.

Women carry fists and anger
compressed under polite smiles
and involuntary tears.

Women carry men
Through…
as they seek healing
from Patriarchy
in softness

they only allow in the
presence of Her.

Women carry groceries to feed families,
carry dishes to potlucks,
carry babies on hips, while
carrying vacuums,
and carrying schedules
of sports games and
conferences and
dentist appointments
and dinner parties.
I once saw a woman
from Burma
at a restaurant in Michigan
cooking while
carrying an infant strapped to
her back.

Women carry their parents into
doctor's appointments
and upstairs,
carry children
overseas,
across borders,
through the desert,
under fences
with barbed wire.

Women carry their sisters
into clinics without judgment,
and hold their hands
through procedures.
Women carry suitcases on
airplanes to walk friends
through chemo, or through divorce,
or through death.

Women carry
sandwiches and humor
to funerals reminding
you to eat and to laugh
and that you will
somehow carry on.

Women
Carry
On.

My Grandmother's Hands

These hands…
These are my grandmother's hands,
bony and brown,
veins bold and blue,
standing at attention.

Hands that traversed the ocean
for the promise of a better life
on Anderdon street
on Detroit's east side.

Hands that applied rouge,
white powder, red lipstick,
teased black hair into
beehives, before nervously
intertwining with my grandfather's
hand on dates chaperoned
by older sister.

Hands that sewed curtains and dresses,
stirred pasta sauce and zucchini stew,
held three babies, thousands of cups of
steaming coffee, and countless
ultra-light cigarettes, while gossiping with
sisters around kitchen tables, with
the Virgin Mary bearing witness from
the olive-green alcove.

These are my grandmother's hands.
What memories do they hold?
What secret longings?
What regrets?

Did a life with so many less options hold more contentment?
Or less?

My world so vastly different
and yet....
and still,

These hands make familiar work...

They, too, are instruments of vanity,
fixing hair and putting on a face.
They, too, make meals to
feed the spirit along with the stomach.
They too caressed crying babies
and carefully built confidence in anxious men.
They too hold cups of coffee,
while sitting quiet in a house that once
held much more noise.
They too rest on kitchen tables,
while trading problems for advice,
wistful and grateful,
as time

rinses it all through fingers
that cannot hold anything
in place.

These hands don't methodically
run over rosary beads,
but they do meet in prayer
and thanksgiving.
They do not sew dresses,
but they do sew tales.
They are hands capable of
catching what comes their way.

These hands…
These are my grandmother's hands.

Lion

You got me old school
daydreaming now,
got me dangerous
now, facing down lions on a
tight rope, no net,
can't maintain my balance,
my grip on your
grey mane got
me imagining
solace in those
lines running criss-
cross from corners
of fiery eyes, full of
faith that should be
long gone. But most
likely, I've got it
all wrong. Let's
get intimate real
quick, so the
fantasy can
pass, cuz my bones,
my bones keep
reminding me
this
ish
won't last.

Do Not Settle for a Teaspoon

Do not settle for a teaspoon
when you are the ocean,
A grain of sand,
when you are as vast as
the desert cradling
Jesus for 40 days.
Don't try to squeeze
a sponge that's been
baking in the sun all day
for a droplet of water to
quench your thirst,
when you have an
icy natural spring bubbling up
in your backyard.

Give compassion,
but not the field of
blazing lavender
that is your soul.

Let them peak out
of their turtle shell
in awe of your courage.
Don't crawl in with them,
live a half-life,
waiting for them to
brave nakedness.

If you show someone the
desert and all they see
is arid land and death,
if they can't see
the magic,
anoint them
with your holy water
and drop them
off at home.

When All Seems Lost

When all we were
building has become
peanut shells under
boots of bullies trying
to stamp us out,
what is there to do?

We throw our arms wide
and wrap them awkwardly
around large oak trees,
press our cheek against
rough bark to remind us
that we were not meant
for these rooms of drywall,
computer screens,
and competition anyway;
Maybe we
were fighting for
a room in a house
we don't even want
to live in. Perhaps, we
let it burn.

Come, lay down in the grass
with me and feel
the damp earth's
embrace;

Remember, kissing
is still free,
and I can
still make a meal
for you, my friend,
and we can listen to horns
in conversation on vinyl,
or see a play that speaks
truth in screams and
whispers. The water
will still rush to meet
our toes in the sand,
and I will still recognize
myself in your tears.

Thank you for reading!

Contact author @ taraling2016@gmail.com

Or follow on IG @taralingeman